DATE DUE

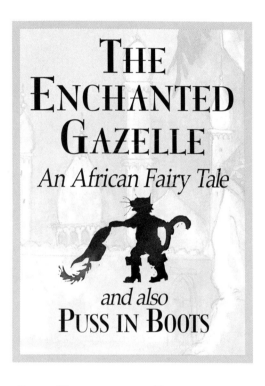

THE ENCHANTED GAZELLE
An African Fairy Tale

and also
PUSS IN BOOTS

by SAVIOUR PIROTTA
and ALAN MARKS

SEA-TO-SEA
Mankato Collingwood London

This edition first published in 2008 by
Sea-to-Sea Publications
1980 Lookout Drive
North Mankato
Minnesota 56003

Text copyright © Saviour Pirotta 2004, 2008
Illustrations copyright © Alan Marks 2004

Printed in China

Library of Congress
Cataloging-in-Publication Data

Pirotta, Saviour.
    The enchanted gazelle/by Saviour Pirotta and Alan Marks
        p.cm. -- (Once upon a world)
    Summary: Presents two tales to compare and contrast, the first from East Africa
featuring a talking gazelle, and the second from France with a talking cat.
    Contents: The enchanted gazelle -- Puss in Boots.
    ISBN 978-1-59771-081-7
        1. Fairy tales. [1. Fairy tales. 2. Folklore.] I. Marks, Alan, 1957-

PZ8.P6672Gaz 2007
[398.2]--dc22

                                        2006053167

9 8 7 6 5 4 3 2

Published by arrangement with the Watts Publishing
Group Ltd, London.

Editor: Rachel Cooke
Series design: Jonathan Hair

Contents

Once upon a time

Animals have been featured in stories since records began. In the great myths of ancient Egypt, Greece, and Rome, the gods often took the shape of animals when they came down to earth. And, today, talking animals appear in many popular children's stories, from *Puss in Boots* (retold at the end of this book) to the *Narnia* stories by C. S. Lewis.

Tales where animals help human beings probably have very ancient origins. Stone Age people painted pictures of the animals they hunted on cave walls and surely told stories about them as well. They depended on these animals for their survival and saw in them abilities which humans did not have.

Tales like *Puss in Boots* are told all over the world, in countries and regions as far afield as Mongolia, Tibet, Siberia, East Africa, Italy, France, Greece, and America. Often the helper is a cat. In some countries it is a fox because foxes, like cats, are considered to be clever and resourceful animals. Animal helper stories differ from country to country but there is one rule that seems to hold true all around the world. Follow the creature's advice and you will prosper beyond your wildest dreams; injure the animal or ignore it and you will live to regret it…

These stories were passed down from generation to generation by word of a mouth, long before anyone wrote them down. *The Enchanted Gazelle*, which you are about to read, is adapted from a story told in Swahili, the language of East Africa.

The Enchanted Gazelle

Once there was a young beggar who had nothing in the world but the tattered robe on his back. His name was Taban. One evening, he was scrabbling through a dust heap looking for stray grains of corn when he found a silver coin. A coin! He held it tightly in his hands, praying he wasn't dreaming. "I could buy myself something special with this," thought Taban.

Just then a pedlar came along the dirt track, pulling behind him an enormous cage on wheels. "Gazelles," he called. "Gazelles for sale."

The entire village came out to have a look.
Taban too approached, the silver coin still
clutched in his hands. "How much do they
cost?" he asked.

The village people burst out laughing.
"Did you hear that?" they said. "That
beggar wants to buy a gazelle."

"And why shouldn't he?" said the pedlar. "Every man should have a companion." He turned to Taban and smiled. "Choose a gazelle, my friend. It will cost you nothing but that little coin in your hand."

One of the animals licked Taban's right hand. "I'll take that one," he said.

Taban tied the gazelle to a tree and, as it was
time to eat, divided his store of corn in two.
The animal, however, refused to eat. "You do
not have enough for yourself," she said.

Taban sprang to his feet. An
animal that spoke! What kind
of wizardry was this?

"There are more things in heaven and earth than you can understand," said the gazelle. "Master, untie me and I shall find my own food. I promise that once my belly is full of grass I shall return."

Taban dared not disobey. He untied her and the enchanted gazelle bounded away into the night. An hour or so later, Taban was woken by a warm tongue licking his face. True to her word, the gazelle had returned.

Taban released the gazelle again on the two nights that followed, but when she did not come back on the third night, he was not surprised. Who would willingly return to be tied to a tree? he thought.

In truth the gazelle had not left him.
While wandering through the dunes behind
the village, she had spied something
glittering in the sand. A diamond!

"This will make master rich," said the
gazelle to herself. Then she thought again.
Would not Taban be taken for a thief if he
tried to sell a jewel?

"I must find another way to help my
master," the gazelle decided.

Taking the diamond in her mouth, she traveled on beyond the dunes into a vast scrubland. After many weeks she caught sight of tall trees in the distance, and mud walls with guards standing on top. She had found a city.

The city streets were bustling with people coming and going. The gazelle dodged in and out of the crowds until she reached a paved square. There, its turrets shimmering in the morning sun, was a sultan's palace.

The gazelle heard that it was the day when the sultan of the city held open court. Anyone could go into his palace to speak to him. The gazelle hurried in, the diamond still hidden in her mouth. When it was her turn to speak, the creature stepped forward gracefully and placed the sparkling diamond at the sultan's feet.

The sultan's jaw dropped. He had never seen a jewel so huge and glittering before. "Who sends this?" he asked.

"My master, the prince Darai," said
the gazelle.

Everyone in the court jumped. A gazelle
that spoke? What kind of wizardry was this?

"There are more things in heaven and earth
than we can understand," said the sultan.

He turned to the gazelle. "And what does

your master want in return for this jewel?"

"The hand of your daughter in marriage," said the gazelle.

"Anyone who possesses such treasures is fit to marry my Princess Amina," said the sultan. "Pray invite your master to my house. He will be most welcome."

The gazelle journeyed across the vast
scrubland once more and found Taban on
the dust heap, still searching for corn.

"Master," she said, "I have found a way
of making you rich beyond your dreams.
You are no longer Taban the beggar but the
Prince Darai, the owner of many treasures."

Once again, Taban dared not disobey. He
followed the gazelle across the scrubland,
braving thirst and thorns, until they reached
the edge of the sultan's city.

There the gazelle told Taban to bathe in
the river. No sooner had the beggar taken
off his robe, than the gazelle picked up a
fallen branch and—Wham! Wham! Wham!

—she beat her master until he lay senseless on the grass. Then, after smearing her face with his blood, she ran to the sultan's palace.

"Your majesty," she gasped, Taban's blood on her snout. "Prince Darai has been set upon by thieves. They've stolen all his clothes and belongings and left him for dead."

The sultan rose to his feet. "Send him a doctor," he ordered. "Take him new clothes too, and a horse to ride into my city."

So Taban, or Prince Darai as he now called
himself, entered the sultan's city dressed in
shimmering finery. The gazelle walked
proudly by his side, her horns held up to the
sky. A few days later the new prince wed
Princess Amina, whose dowry of lace and
jewels filled two entire rooms.

Yet the gazelle could not rest. "Master," she said, "you are now a rich man but you do not have your own palace or kingdom. Let me find them for you."

Once more the enchanted creature set out on her quest. This time, she traveled up into the mountains that rose in misted peaks behind the sultan's kingdom. She came to a

small city on a
plateau, but its
houses weren't grand
enough for a new prince
and his beloved wife so the
gazelle journeyed on.

One morning, she saw to a dusty palace
some distance from the city. It must have
been beautiful once but now it looked
neglected. The mud was
falling off the walls
and swallows had
built their nests in
the wooden
balconies. The
gazelle knocked
on the door.

"You'd best be on your way," said a quavering voice, "or you shall suffer the most dreadful agonies."

The gazelle answered, "Whatever trouble you are in, I can save you."

The door opened and a woman peeped out. "This house belongs to a huge serpent," she said. "He has seven heads. Seven barrels of meat a day he devours, and seven more of water. It takes me and the other slaves here a whole day to fill them up. But does he thank us? No. The moment he has eaten, the brute disappears again. No one knows where he goes."

"Is the serpent feeding now?" asked the gazelle.

"No," answered the woman. "He has not yet come home."

"And does your master have a sword?"
asked the gazelle.

"He keeps it in a chest under the stairs,"
replied the woman. "Its blade is so sharp, it
can cut through stone."

"Fetch it," said the gazelle, "and I shall set
you all free."

The woman had hardly let the gazelle into the palace and fetched the sword when a strange wind started howling around the palace. The stench of rotting meat filled the air. Then the serpent appeared, filling the courtyard with monstrous shiny coils. He started to eat at once, each head lapping away at one of the seven pots. When he had finished the meat, he turned to the water jars.

"What's that smell?" he roared suddenly, deafening the woman with his seven voices. "Is there a stranger in the house?"

"No," replied the woman, "it's just a new perfume I made."

"You're lying," said the serpent. "There's someone in my house."

The beast started crawling toward the door, his seven heads peering around, flicking their forked tongues. The gazelle was waiting for him. The moment the first head came through the door, she lashed out with the sword. "Woman, was that a splinter of wood from the door that scratched my neck?"asked the serpent.

"It was," lied the woman.

The second head came through the door and the gazelle struck again.

"Woman, was that a nail that scratched me?" asked the serpent.

"It was," lied the woman again.

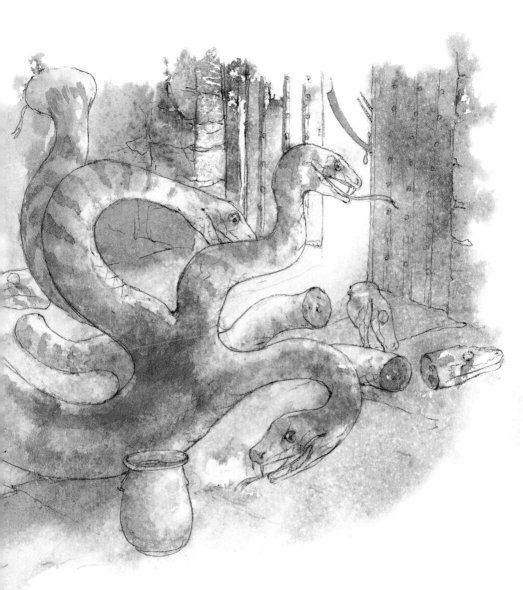

The gazelle hit out with the sword four
more times. Each time, the blade sliced
through the serpent's flesh so cleanly, he
could not tell he was losing a head.

When there was only the seventh head
left, the gazelle stepped from behind the
door and the monster finally saw what was
happening. He roared and fire came out of
his mouth but most of his strength had
oozed away with his blood.
One more strike of the
sword and the gazelle had
killed the beast.

The slaves in the palace
cheered. "You are now
our master," they said.
"This palace and all its
treasures are yours."

"I do not want
anything for
myself," said the
gazelle. "I shall
fetch my master
and his bride."

A few weeks later, Prince Darai and
Princess Amina were living in their new
palace, which they set about repairing.
Half of the sultan's court came to live with
them, for all wanted to be close to the
enchanted gazelle.

The Prince Darai should have been
content. He was no longer a beggar but a

rich prince whose wife loved and adored
him. Yet he was not happy. The people
around him did not respect him as much as
the gazelle. It was her they turned to for
advice; it was her they asked to recount
stories around the fire.

The prince was consumed with jealousy,
and began to hate the gazelle.

The gazelle was unhappy, too. "My master has not even thanked me for all that I have done for him," she thought. And, in her sorrow, she refused to eat, even when the servants brought her the fresh grass she liked so much.

One day the servants came to Prince Darai with sad news. "The gazelle is unwell," they said.

"Give her soup with millet, 'said the prince, "that will make her feel better."

"The doctor said she needs a potion with milk and ground rice," said the servants.

"We don't want to waste rice on animals," argued the prince.

"Give her some millet. If it's good enough for my horses, it should be good enough for a gazelle."

When the gazelle heard what the prince had said, tears rolled down her furry cheeks. She turned her horns to the sky and let out a sigh. "She is dead," said the doctor, closing her eyes.

A great wailing echoed around the palace. Servants and stable hands, cooks, and courtiers, everyone cried and the women, led by Princess Amina, tore the scarves from their heads. Only Prince Darai remained unmoved. He had the gazelle's body thrown down a well.

"You insult the gazelle's memory," said
Princess Amina. "You are not a prince, but
an ignorant and selfish
man who does not
deserve my love."

That night, the princess dreamt she was back in her father's palace. A great feast was in progress and the guest of honor was the enchanted gazelle, not dead but alive and as beautiful as ever. When the princess woke up, she found that her dream had come true.

Prince Darai had a dream, too. In it he was no longer a prince but a beggar in a tattered robe, looking for corn in the dust heap. When he woke up, he felt the sun on his back and dust trickling through his fingers. His dream had come true as well.

Puss in Boots

Puss in Boots is one of the most popular of the many stories collected by French storyteller Charles Perrault. He adapted it from a French folk tale at the very end of the 17th century. He made one significant change from his source—he made his cat male. In most similar stories, the magical animal helper is female.

Once there was an old miller who died, leaving something to each of his three sons. The eldest inherited the mill, the second got a donkey, and the youngest was given a cat. "My brothers can make a living out of their inheritance," said the youngest to himself, "but how am I supposed to live off a cat?"

"Give me a drawstring bag and a pair of boots," said the cat, who could talk. "You'll soon find out that I am worth much more than a mill or a stupid donkey."

The young man did as he was asked, even though he did not believe a single word the cat said. He'd never seen him do anything except chase mice when he was hungry.

The cat put on the boots and tucked some bran in the bag. Then he used the bag to trap a fat, foolish rabbit that was lured into it by the bran.

The cat took the rabbit not to his master but to the king. "Sire," the cat said, "my master, the Marquis of Carabas, wishes to give you this rabbit he has caught."

"Tell your master I am greatly pleased with his gift," said the king.

The next morning the cat went hunting again. This time he caught a brace of partridges.

Again he took his catch to the king. "More gifts from my lord, the Marquis of Carabas," he announced. And again, the king thanked him and sent greetings to the generous marquis.

For the next three months, Puss in Boots, as people now called him, came to the palace often, bringing more gifts from his master. One day, he learnt that the king and his daughter were going for a ride along the river.

Puss in Boots bolted home. "Master," he said to the miller's son. "If you follow my advice your fortune is made. Go and wash yourself in the river, by the old apple tree."

The miller's son did what Puss in Boots advised. While he was bathing, the king's carriage came rattling by.

"Help, help," shouted Puss in Boots,

leaping out from behind the tree. "My Lord Marquis of Carabas has been attacked by thieves. They have thrown him in the river."

The king ordered the coachman to stop. He put his head out of the carriage window and saw his friend Puss in Boots. "Quick!" he said. "Pull the marquis out of the river and give him some clothes."

The servants rescued the miller's son and, as Puss in Boots had hidden his clothes, they gave him an elegant suit to put on. The young man looked so handsome in his new finery that the king's daughter fell in love with him.

The king invited the marquis to ride in the carriage with him and the royal party moved on, the cat walking ahead of it. Soon they came to a meadow that belonged to an ogre. Farmworkers were mowing the grass. The cat said to them: "Good people, tell the king that this meadow belongs to the Lord Marquis of Carabas or my master will have you chopped like herbs for the pot." The king stopped the carriage and leaned out of the window. "Who does this meadow belong to?" he asked.

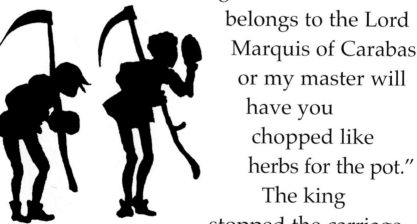

"To the Lord Marquis of Carabas," chorused the farmworkers.

The carriage came to another field, which also belonged to the ogre. Puss in Boots had

worked the same trickery. When the king asked the farm workers who the land belonged to, they all said: "To the Lord Marquis of Carabas." The king had no reason to doubt them.

Meanwhile, Puss in Boots hurried on until he came to the ogre's castle. He knocked on the door and said he'd come to pay his respects. The ogre let him in and, never having met a cat who wore boots before, offered him some wine.

"I have been told," said the cat, "that you can change shape at will—into a lion or an elephant, for example."

"That is true," answered the ogre. And he changed into a lion to prove his point.

"I've also heard," said Puss in Boots when the ogre had returned to his natural form, "that you can take the shape of the smallest creatures, like mice and birds. Pardon me for being so rude, but surely such a big person cannot become something so small."

"Do you doubt my powers?" roared the ogre. And he turned into a small mouse, scurrying around the floor. Puss in Boots leapt on him and, in an instant swallowed him up. Then he ran out of the castle to greet the king's carriage. "Your Majesty," he called, "welcome to the home of my Lord Marquis of Carabas."

"Does this belong to you as well?" said the king to the marquis. "There is no finer castle in the land. Pray, let me have a look inside."

The Marquis of Carabas gave his hand to the princess and followed the king into the castle, where they found the table laid with a rich feast for the ogre. The king was so impressed that he whispered to his daughter, "You could do worse than choose this man for your husband."

"Oh, father," said the princess, "can we marry right away? The marquis and I are very much in love."

The wedding took place a few days later. Puss became a great lord, and he never again had to run after mice for his dinner—but only chased them for a bit of fun.

Taking it further

Once you've read both stories in this book, there is lots more you can think and talk about. There's plenty to write about, too.

• To begin with, think about what is the same and what is different about the two stories. Talk about these with other people. Which story do you prefer and why?

• Imagine you are your favorite animal. What would your special powers be? How would you use them to help other people? Write and illustrate a comic featuring your animal-self as the hero.

• Get together with some friends. Each person chooses a character from one or other of the stories. Now invite each person to retell the story from the point of view of their character. You could use these to develop a play based on the story.

• Find ancient Greek or Egyptian myths that feature animal helpers. Draw pictures of them and create an animal gallery. You could also include other magical animal characters you know.